Libbie Marsh's Three Eras

Elizabeth Gaskell

Table of Contents

Libbie Marsh's Three Eras

Elizabeth Gaskell

ERA I. VALENTINE'S DAY

Last November but one, there was a flitting in our neighbourhood; hardly a flitting, after all, for it was only a single person changing her place of abode from one lodging to another; and instead of a cartload of drawers and baskets, dressers and beds, with old king clock at the top of all, it was only one large wooden chest to be carried after the girl, who moved slowly and heavily along the streets, listless and depressed, more from the state of her mind than of her body. It was Libbie Marsh, who had been obliged to quit her room in Dean Street, because the acquaintances whom she had been living with were leaving Manchester. She tried to think herself fortunate in having met with lodgings rather more out of the town, and with those who were known to be respectable; she did indeed try to be contented, but in spite of her reason, the old feeling of desolation came over her, as she was now about to be thrown again entirely among strangers.

No. 2. — Court, Albemarle Street, was reached at last, and the pace, slow as it was, slackened as she drew near the spot where she was to be left by the man who carried her box, for, trivial as her acquaintance with him was, he was not quite a stranger, as everyone else was, peering out of their open doors, and satisfying themselves it was only 'Dixon's new lodger.'

Dixon's house was the last on the left–hand side of the court. A high dead brick wall connected it with its opposite neighbour. All the dwellings were of the same monotonous pattern, and one side of the court looked at its exact likeness opposite, as if it were seeing itself in a looking–glass.

Dixon's house was shut up, and the key left next door; but the woman in whose charge it was left knew that Libbie was expected, and came forward to say a few explanatory words, to unlock the door, and stir the dull grey ashes that were lazily burning in the grate: and then she returned to her own house, leaving poor Libbie standing alone with the great big chest in the middle of the house–place floor, with no one to say a word to (even a commonplace remark would have been better than this dull silence), that could help her to repel the fast–coming tears.

Dixon and his wife, and their eldest girl, worked in factories, and were absent all day from the house: the youngest child, also a little girl, was boarded out on the week–days at the neighbour's where the door–key was deposited, but although busy making, dirt–pies, at the entrance to the court, when Libbie came in, she was too young to care much about her parents' new lodger. Libbie knew that she was to sleep with the elder girl in the front bedroom, but, as you may fancy, it seemed a liberty even to go upstairs to take off her things, when no one was at home to marshal the way up the ladder–like steps. So she could only take off her bonnet, and sit down, and gaze at the now blazing fire, and think sadly on the past, and on the lonely creature she was in this wide world—father and mother gone, her little brother long since dead—he would have been more than nineteen had he been alive, but she only thought of him as the darling baby; her only friends (to call friends) living far away at their new house; her employers, kind enough people in their way, but too rapidly twirling round on this bustling earth to have leisure to think of the little work–woman, excepting when they wanted gowns turned, carpets mended, or household linen darned; and hardly even the natural though hidden hope of a young girl's heart, to cheer her on with the bright visions of a home of her own at some future day, where, loving and beloved, she might fulfil a woman's dearest duties.

For Libbie was very plain, as she had known so long that the consciousness of it had ceased to mortify her. You can hardly live in Manchester without having some idea of your personal appearance: the factory lads and lasses take good care of that; and if you meet them at the hours when they are pouring out of the mills, you are sure to hear a good number of truths, some of them combined with such a spirit of impudent fun, that you can scarcely keep from laughing, even at the joke against yourself Libbie had often and often been greeted by such questions as—'How long is it since you were a beauty?'—'What would you take a day to stand in the fields to scare away the birds?' for her to linger under any impression as to her looks.

While she was thus musing, and quietly crying, under the pictures her fancy had conjured up, the Dixons came dropping in, and surprised her with her wet cheeks and quivering lips.

She almost wished to have the stillness again that had so oppressed her an hour ago, they talked and laughed so loudly and so much, and bustled about so noisily over everything they did. Dixon took hold of one iron handle of her box, and helped her to bump it upstairs, while his daughter Anne followed to see the unpacking, and what sort of clothes 'little sewing body had gotten.' Mrs Dixon rattled out her tea–things, and put the kettle on, fetched home her youngest child, which added to the commotion. Then she called

3

Libbie Marsh's Three Eras

Anne downstairs, and sent her for this thing and that: eggs to put to the cream, it was so thin; barn, to give a relish to the bread and butter; some new bread, hot, if she could get it. Libbie heard all these orders, given at full pitch of Mrs Dixon's voice, and wondered at their extravagance, so different from the habits of the place where she had last lodged. But they were fine spinners, in the receipt of good wages; and confined all day in an atmosphere ranging from seventy–five to eighty degrees. They had lost all natural, healthy appetite for simple food, and, having no higher tastes, found their greatest enjoyment in their luxurious meals.

When tea was ready, Libbie was called downstairs, with a rough but hearty invitation, to share their meal; she sat mutely at the corner of the tea–table, while they went on with their own conversation about people and things she knew nothing about, till at length she ventured to ask for a candle, to go and finish her unpacking before bedtime, as she had to go our sewing for several succeeding days. But once in the comparative peace of her bedroom, her energy failed her, and she contented herself with locking her Noah's ark of a chest, and put out her candle, and went to sit by the window, and gaze our at the bright heavens; for ever and ever 'the blue sky, that bends over all,' sheds down a feeling of sympathy with the sorrowful at the solemn hours when, the ceaseless stars are seen to pace its depths.

By–and–by her eye fell down to gazing at the corresponding window to her own, on the opposite side of the court. It was lighted, but the blind was drawn down: upon the blind she saw, first unconsciously, the constant weary motion of a little spectral shadow, a child's hand and arm—no more; long, thin fingers hanging down from the wrist, while the arm moved up and down, as if keeping time to the heavy pulses of dull, pain. She could not help hoping that sleep would soon come to still that incessant, feeble, motion: and now and then it did cease, as if the little creature had dropped into a slumber from very weariness; but presently the arm jerked up with the fingers clenched, as if with a sudden start of agony. When Anne came up to bed, Libbie was still sitting, watching the shadow, and she directly asked to whom it belonged.

'It will be Margaret Hall's lad. Last summer, when it was so hot, there was no biding with the window shut at night, and theirs was open too: and many's the time he has waked me with his moans; they say he's been better sin' cold weather came.'

'Is he always in bed? Whatten ails him?' asked Libbie.

4

Libbie Marsh's Three Eras

'Summat's amiss wi' his backbone, folks say; he's better and worse, like. He's a nice little chap enough, and his mother's nor that bad either; only my mother and her had words, so now we don't speak.'

Libbie went on watching, and when she next spoke, to ask who and what his mother was, Anne Dixon was fast asleep.

Time passed away, and as usual unveiled the hidden things. Libbie found out that Margaret Hall was a widow, who earned her living as a washerwoman; that the little suffering lad was her only child, her dearly beloved. That while she scolded, pretty nearly, everybody else, 'till her name was up' in the neighbourhood for a termagant, to him she was evidently most tender and gentle. He lay alone on his little bed, near the window, through the day, while she was away toiling for a livelihood. But when Libbie had plain sewing to do at her lodgings, instead of going out to sew, she used to watch from her bedroom window for the time when the shadows opposite, by their mute gestures, told that the mother had returned to bend over her child, to smooth his pillow, to alter his position, to get him his nightly cup of tea. And often in the night Libbie could not help rising gently from bed, to see if the little arm was waving up and down, as was his accustomed habit when sleepless from pain.

Libbie had a good deal of sewing to do at borne that winter, and whenever it was not so cold as to benumb her fingers, she took it upstairs, in order to watch the little lad in her few odd moments of pause. On his better days he could sit up enough to peep out of his window, and she found he liked to look at her. Presently she ventured to nod to him across the court; and his faint smile, and ready nod back again, showed that this gave him pleasure. I think she would have been encouraged by this smile to have proceeded to a speaking acquaintance, if it had not been for, his terrible mother, to whom it seemed to be irritation enough to know that Libbie was a lodger at the Dixons' for her to talk at her whenever they encountered each other, and to live evidently in wait for some good opportunity of abuse.

With her constant interest in him, Libbie soon discovered his great want of an object on which to occupy his thoughts, and which might distract his attention, when alone through the long day, from the pain he endured. He was very fond of flowers. It was November when she had first removed to her lodgings, but it had been very mild weather, and a few flowers yet lingered in the gardens, which the country people gathered into nosegays, and brought on market–days into Manchester. His mother had bought him a bunch of Michaelmas daisies the very day Libbie had become a neighbour, and she watched their history. He put them first in an old teapot, of which the spout was broken off and the lid lost; and he daily replenished the teapot from the jug of water his mother left near him to quench his feverish thirst. By–and–by, one or two of the constellation of lilac stars faded, and then the time he had hitherto spent in admiring, almost caressing them, was devoted to cutting off those flowers whose decay marred the beauty of the nosegay. It cook him half the morning, with his feeble, languid motions, and his cumbrous old scissors, to trim up big diminished darlings. Then at last he seemed to think he had better preserve the few that remained by drying them; so they were carefully put between the leaves of the old Bible; and then, whenever a better day came, when he had strength enough to lift the ponderous book, he used to open the pages to look at his flower friends. In winter he could have no more living flowers to tend.

Libbie thought and thought, till at last an idea flashed upon her mind, that often made a happy smile steal over her face as she stitched away and that cheered her through the solitary winter—for solitary it continued to be, though the Dixons were very good sort of people, never pressed her for payment, if she had had but little–work to do that week; never grudged her a share of their extravagant meals, which were far more luxurious than she could have met with anywhere else, for her previously agreed payment in case of working at home; and they would fain have taught her to drink rum in her tea, assuring her that she should have it for nothing and welcome. But they were too touchy, too prosperous, too much absorbed in themselves, to take off Libbie's feeling of solitariness; not half as much as the little face by day, and the shadow by night, of him with whom she had never yet exchanged a word.

Her idea was this: her mother came from the cast of England, where, as perhaps you know, they have the pretty custom of sending presents on St Valentine's day, with the donor's name unknown, and, of course, the mystery constitutes half the enjoyment. The fourteenth of February was Libbie's birthday too, and many a year, in the happy days of old. had, her mother delighted to surprise her with some little gift, of which she more than half–guessed the giver, although each Valentine's day the manner of its arrival was varied. Since then the fourteenth of February had been the dreariest of all the year, because the most haunted by memory of departed happiness. But now, this year, if she could not have the old gladness of heart herself, she would try and brighten the life of another. She would save, and she would screw, but she would buy a canary and a cage for that poor little laddie opposite, who wore out his monotonous life with so few pleasures, and so much pain.

I doubt I may not tell you here of the anxieties and the fears, of the hopes and the self—sacrifice—all, perhaps small in the tangible effect as the widow's mite, yet not the less marked by the viewless angels who go about continually among us—which varied Libbie's life before she accomplished her purpose. It is enough to say it was accomplished. The very day before the fourteenth she found time to go with her half—guinea to a barber's who lived near Albemarle Street, and who was famous for his stock of singing—birds. There are enthusiasts about all sorts of things, both good and bad, and many of the weavers in Manchester know and care more about birds than anyone would easily credit. Stubborn, silent, reserved men on many things, you have only to touch on the subject of birds to light up their faces with brightness. They will tell you who won the prizes at the last canary show, where the prize birds may be seen, and give you all the details of those funny, but pretty and interesting mimicries of great people's cattle shows. Among these amateurs, Emanuel Morris the barber was an oracle.

He took Libbie into his little back room, used for private shaving of modest men, who did not care to be exhibited in the front shop decked out in the full glories of lather; and which was hung round with birds in rude wicker cages, with the exception of those who had won prizes, and were consequently honoured with gilt—wire prisons. The longer and thinner the body of the bird was, the more admiration it received, as far as external beauty went; and when, in addition to this, the colour was deep and clear, and its notes strong and varied, the more did Emanuel dwell upon its perfections. But these were all prize birds, and, on inquiry, Libbie heard, with some little sinking at heart, that their price ran from one to two guineas.

'I'm not over—particular as to shape and colour,' said she, 'I should like a good singer, that's all!'

She dropped a little in Emanuel's estimation. However, he showed her his good singers, but all were above Libbie's means.

'After all, I don't think I care so much about the singing very loud; it's but a noise after all, and sometimes noise fidgets folks.'

'They must be nesh folks as is put out with the singing o' birds,' replied Emanuel, rather affronted.

'It's for one who is poorly,' said Libbie, deprecatingly.

'Well,' said he, as if considering the matter, 'folk that are cranky, often take more to them as shows 'em love, than to them as is clever and gifted. Happen yo'd rather have this'n,' opening a cage–door, and calling to a dull–coloured bird, sitting moped up in a corner, 'Here—Jupiter, Jupiter!'

The bird smoothed its feathers in an instant, and, uttering a little note of delight, flew to Emanuel, putting his beak to his lips, as if kissing him, and then, perching on his head, it began a gurgling warble of pleasure, not by any means so varied or so clear as the song of the others, but which pleased Libbie more; for she was always one to find out she liked the gooseberries that were accessible, better than the grapes that were beyond her reach. The price too was just right, so she gladly cook possession of the cage, and hid it under her cloak, preparatory to carrying it home. Emanuel meanwhile was giving her directions as to its food, with all the, minuteness of one loving his subject.

'Will it soon get to know anyone?' asked she.

'Give him two days only, and you and he'll be as thick as him and me are now. You've only to open his door, and call him, and he'll follow you round the room; but he'll first kiss you, and then perch on your head. He only wants larning, which I've no time to give him, to do many another accomplishment.'

'What's his name? I did not rightly catch it.'

'Jupiter,—it's not common; but, the town's o'errun with Bobbies and Dickies, and as my birds are thought a bit our o' the way, I like to have better names for 'em, so I just picked a few out o' my lad's school books. It's just as ready, when you're used to it, to say Jupiter as Dicky.'

'I could bring my tongue round to Peter better; would he answer to Peter?' asked Libbie, now on the point of departing.

Libbie Marsh's Three Eras

'Happen he might; but I think he'd come readier to the three syllables.'

On Valentine's day, Jupiter's cage was decked round with ivy leaves, making quite a pretty wreath on the wicker work; and to one of them was pinned a slip of paper, with these words, written in Libbie's best round hand:—

'From your faithful Valentine. Please take notice his name is Peter, and he'll come if you call him, after a bit.'

But little work did Libbie do that afternoon, she was so engaged in watching for the messenger who was to bear her present to her little valentine, and run away as soon as he had delivered up the canary, and explained to whom it was sent.

At last he came; then there was a pause before the woman of the house was at liberty to take it upstairs. Then Libbie saw the little face flush up into a bright colour, the feeble bands tremble with delighted eagerness, the head bent down to try and make our the writing (beyond his power, poor lad, to read), the rapturous turning round of the cage in order to see the canary in every point of view, head, tail, wings, and feet; an intention in which Jupiter, in his uneasiness at being again among strangers, did nor second, for he hopped round so as continually to present a full front to the boy. It was a source of never wearying delight to the little fellow, till daylight closed in; he evidently forgot to wonder who had sent it him, in his gladness at his possession of such a treasure; and when the shadow of his mother darkened on the blind, and the bird had been exhibited, Libbie saw her do what, with all her tenderness, seemed rarely to have entered into her thoughts he bent down and kissed her boy, in a mother's sympathy with the joy of her child.

The canary was placed for the night between the little bed and window; and when Libbie rose once, to take her accustomed peep, she saw the little arm put fondly round the cage, as if embracing his new treasure even in his sleep. How Jupiter slept this first night is quite another thing.

So ended the first day in Libbie's three ems in last year.

ERA II. WHITSUNTIDE

The brightest, fullest daylight poured down into No. 2, — Court, Albemarle Street, and the heat, even at the early hour of five, as at the noontide on the June days of many years past.

The court seemed alive, and merry with voices and laughter. The bedroom windows were open wide, and had been so all night, on account of the heat; and every now and then you might see a head and a pair of shoulders, simply encased in shirt sleeves, popped out, and you might hear the inquiry passed from one to the other,—'Well, jack, and where art thee bound for?'

'Dunham!'

'Why, what an old–fashioned chap thou be'st. Thy grandad afore thee went to Dunham: but thou wert always a slow coach. I'm off to Alderley, – me and my missis.'

'Ay, that's because there's only thee and thy missis. Wait till thou hast gotten four childer, like me, and thou'lt he glad enough to take 'em to Dunham, oud–fashioned way, for fourpence apiece.'

'I'd still go to Alderley; I'd not he bothered with my children; they should keep house at home.'

A pair of hands, the person to whom they belonged invisible, boxed his cars on this last speech, in a very spirited, though playful, manner, and the neighbours all laughed at the surprised look of the speaker, at this assault from an unseen foe. The man who had been holding conversation with him cried out,—

'Sarved him right, Mrs Slater: he knows nought about it yet; but when he gets them he'll be as loth to leave the babbies at home on a Whitsuntide as any on us. We shall live to see him in Dunham Park yet, wi' twins in his arms, and another pair on 'em clutching at daddy's coat–tails, let alone your share of youngsters, missis.'

At this moment our friend Libbie appeared at her window, and Mrs Slater, who had taken her discomfited husband's place, called out,—

'Elizabeth Marsh, where are Dixons and you bound to?'

'Dixons are not up yet; he said last night he'd take his holiday out in lying in bed. I'm going to the old–fashioned place, Dunham.'

'Thou art never going by thyself, moping!'

'No. I'm going with Margaret Hall and her lad,' replied Libbie, hastily withdrawing from the window, in order to avoid hearing any remarks on the associates she had chosen for her day of pleasure—the scold of the neighbourhood, and her sickly, ailing child!

But Jupiter might have been a dove, and his ivy leaves an olive branch, for the peace he had brought, the happiness he had caused, to three individuals at least. For of course it could not long be a mystery who had sent little Frank Hall his valentine; nor could his mother long entertain her hard manner towards one who had given her child a new pleasure. She was shy, and she was proud, and for some time she struggled against the natural desire of manifesting her gratitude; but one evening, when Libbie was returning home, with a bundle of work half as large as herself, as she dragged herself along through the heated streets, she was overtaken by Margaret Hall, her burden gently pulled from her, and her way home shortened, and her weary spirits soothed and cheered, by the outpourings of Margaret's heart; for the barrier of reserve once broken down, she had much to say, to thank her for days of amusement and happy employment for her lad, to speak of his gratitude, to tell of her hopes and fears,—the hopes and fears that made up the dates of her life. From that time, Libbie lost her awe of the termagant in interest for the mother, whose all was ventured in so frail a bark. From this time, Libbie was a fast friend with both mother and son, planning mitigations for the sorrowful days of the latter as eagerly as poor Margaret Hall, and with far more success. His life had flickered up under the charm and excitement of the last few months. He even seemed strong enough to undertake the journey to Dunham, which Libbie had arranged as a Whitsuntide treat, and for which she and his mother had been hoarding up for several weeks. The canal boat left Knott Mill at six, and it was now past five; so Libbie let herself out very gently, and went across to her friends. She knocked at the door of their lodging–room, and, without waiting for an answer, entered.

Franky's face was flushed, and he was trembling with excitement,— partly with pleasure, but partly with some eager wish not yet granted.

'He wants sore to take Peter with him,' said his mother to Libbie, as if referring the matter to her. The boy looked imploringly at her.

'He would like it, I know; for one thing, he'd miss me sadly, and chirrup for me all day long, he'd be so lonely. I could not be half so happy a–thinking on him, left alone here by himself. Then, Libbie, he's just like a Christian, so fond of flowers and green leaves, and them sort of things. He chirrups to me so when mother brings me a pennyworth of wallflowers to put round his cage. He would talk if he could, you know; but I can tell what he means quite as one as if he spoke. Do let Peter go, Libbie; I'll carry him in my own arms.'

So Jupiter was allowed to be of the party. Now Libbie had overcome the great difficulty of conveying Franky to the boat, by offering to 'slay' for a coach, and the shouts and exclamations of the neighbours told them that their conveyance awaited them at the bottom of the court. His mother carried Franky, light in weight, though heavy in helplessness, and he would hold the cage believing that he was thus redeeming his pledge, that Peter should be a trouble to no one. Libbie proceeded to arrange the bundle containing their dinner, as a support in the corner of the coach. The neighbours came out with many blunt speeches, and more kindly wishes, and one or two of them would have relieved Margaret of her burden, if she would have allowed it. The presence of that little crippled fellow seemed to obliterate all the angry feelings which had existed between his mother and her neighbours, and which had formed the politics of that little court for many a day.

And now they were fairly off! Franky bit his lips in attempted endurance of the pain the motion caused him; he winced and shrank until they were fairly on a Macadamized thoroughfare, when e closed his eyes, and seemed desirous of a few minutes' rest. Libbie fell very shy, and very much afraid of being seen by her employers, 'set up in a coach!' and so she hid herself in a corner, and made herself as small as possible; while Mrs Hall had exactly the opposite feeling, and was delighted to stand up, stretching out of the window, and nodding to pretty nearly everyone they met or passed on the footpaths; and they were not a few, for the streets were quite gay, even at that early hour, with parties going to this or that railway station, or to the boats which crowded the canals on this bright holiday week; and almost everyone they met seemed to enter into Mrs Hall's exhilaration of feeling, and had a smile or nod in return. At last she plumped down by Libbie, and exclaimed, 'I never was in a coach but once afore, and that was when I was a-going to be married. It's like heaven; and all done over with such beautiful gimp, too!' continued she, admiring the lining of the vehicle. Jupiter did not enjoy it so much.

As if the holiday time, the lovely weather, and the 'sweet hour of prime' had a genial influence, as no doubt they have, everybody's heart seemed softened towards poor Franky. The driver lifted him out with the tenderness of strength, and bore him carefully down to the boat; the people then made way, and gave him the best seat in their power,—or rather I should call it a couch, for they saw he was weary, and insisted on his lying down,—an attitude he would have been ashamed to assume without the protection of his mother and Libbie, who now appeared, bearing their baskets and carrying Peter.

Away the boat went, to make room for others, for every conveyance, both by land and water, is in requisition in Whitsun- week, to give the hard-worked crowds the opportunity of enjoying the charms of the country. Even every standing-place in the canal packets was occupied, and as they glided along, the banks were lined with people, who seemed to find it object enough to watch the boats go by, packed close and full with happy beings brimming with anticipations of a day's pleasure. The country through which they passed is as uninteresting as can well be imagined; but still it is the country: and the screams of delight from the children, and the low laughs of pleasure from the parents. at every blossoming tree that trailed its wreath against some cottage wall, or at the tufts of late primroses which lingered in the cool depths of grass along the canal banks, the thorough relish of everything, as if dreading to let the least circumstance of this happy day pass over without its due appreciation, made the time seem all too short, although it took two hours to arrive at a place only eight miles from Manchester. Even Franky, with all his impatience to see Dunham woods (which I think he confused with London, believing both to be paved with gold), enjoyed the easy motion of the boat so much, floating along, while pictures moved before him, that he regretted when the time came for landing among the soft, green meadows, that came sloping down to the dancing water's brim. His fellow-passengers carried him to the park, and refused all payment, although his mother had laid by sixpence on purpose, as a recompense for this service.

'Oh, Libbie, how beautiful! Oh, mother, mother! is the whole world our of Manchester as beautiful as this? I did not know trees were like this! Such green homes for, birds! Look,

Libbie Marsh's Three Eras

Peter! would not you like to he there, up among those boughs? But I can't let you go, you know, because you're my little bird brother, and I should be quite lost without you.'

They spread a shawl upon the fine mossy turf, at the root of a beech–tree, which made a sort of natural couch, and there they laid him, and bade him rest, in spite of the delight which made him believe himself capable of any exertion. Where he lay,—always holding Jupiter's cage, and often talking to him as to a playfellow,—he was on the verge of a green area, shut in by magnificent trees, in all the glory of their early foliage, before the summer heats had deepened their verdure into one rich, monotonous tint. And hither came party after party; old men and maidens, young men and, children,—whole families trooped along after the, guiding fathers, who bore the youngest in their arms, or astride upon their backs, while they turned round occasionally to the wives, with whom they shared some fond local remembrance. For years has Dunham Park been the favourite resort of the Manchester workpeople; for more years than I can tell; probably ever since 'the Duke,' by his canals, opened out the system of cheap travelling. Its scenery, too, which presents such a complete contrast to the whirl and turmoil of Manchester; so thoroughly–woodland, with its ancestral trees (here and there lightning blanched); its 'verdurous walls;' its grassy walks, leading far away into, some glade, where you start at the rabbit rustling among the last year's fern, and where the wood–pigeon's call seems the only fitting and accordant sound. Depend upon it, this complete sylvan repose, this accessible quiet, this lapping the soul in green images of the country, forms the most, complete contrast; to a town's–person, and consequently has over suck the greatest power to charm.

Presently Libbie found our she was very hungry. Now they were but provided with dinner, which was, of course, to be eaten as near twelve o'clock as might be; and Margaret Hall, in her prudence, asked a working–man near to tell her what o'clock it was.

'Nay,' said he, 'I'll ne'er look at clock or watch today. I'll not spoil my pleasure by finding out how fast it's going away. If thou'rt hungry, eat. I make my own dinner hour, and I have eaten, mine an hour ago.'

So they had their veal pies, and then found out it was only about half–past ten o'clock; by so many pleasurable events had that morning been marked. But such was their buoyancy of spirits, that they only enjoyed their mistake, and joined in the general laugh against the man who had eaten his dinner somewhere about nine. He laughed most heartily of all, till, suddenly stopping, he said,—

'I must not go on at this rate; laughing gives one such an appetite.'

'Oh! if that's all,' said a merry–looking man, lying at full length, and brushing the fresh scent out of the grass, while two or three little children tumbled over him, and crept about him, as kittens or puppies frolic with their parents, 'if that's all, we'll have a subscription of eatables for them improvident folk as have eaten their dinner for their breakfast. Here's a sausage pasty and a handful of nuts for my share. Bring round a hat, Bob, and see what the company will give.'

Bob carried out the joke, much to little Franky's amusement; and no one was so churlish as to refuse, although the contributions varied from a peppermint drop up to a veal pie, and a sausage pasty.

'It's a thriving trade,' said Bob, as be emptied his hatful of provisions on the grass by Libbie's side. 'Besides, it's tiptop, too, to live on the public. Hark! what is that?'

The laughter and the chat were suddenly hushed, and mothers told their little ones to listen,—as, far away in the distance, now sinking and falling, now swelling and clear, came a ringing peal of children's voices, blended together in one of those psalm tunes which we are all of us familiar with, and which bring to mind the old, old days, when we, as wondering children, were first led to worship 'Our Father,' by those beloved ones who have since gone to the more perfect worship. Holy was that distant choral praise, even to the most thoughtless; and when it, in fact, was ended, in the instant's pause, during which the ear awaits the repetition of the air, they caught the noontide hum and buzz of the myriads of insects who danced away their lives in the glorious day; they heard the swaying of the mighty woods in the soft but resistless breeze, and then again once more burst forth the merry jests and the shouts of childhood; and again the elder ones resumed their happy talk, as they lay or sat 'under the greenwood tree.' Fresh parties came dropping in; some laden jwith wild flowers— almost with branches of hawthorn, indeed; while one or two had made prizes of the earliest dog–roses, and had cast away campion, stitchwort, ragged robin, all to keep the lady of the hedges from being obscured or hidden by the community.

One after another drew near to Franky, and looked on with interest as he lay sorting the flowers given to him. Happy parents stood by, with their household bands around them, in health and comeliness, and felt the sad prophecy of those shrivelled limbs, those wasted fingers, those lamp−like eyes, with their bright, dark lustre. His mother was too eagerly watching his happiness to read the meaning of those grave looks, but Libbie saw them and understood them; and a chill shudder went through her, even on that day, as she thought on the future.

'Ay! I thought we should give you a start!'

A start they did give, with their terrible slap on Libbie's back, as she sat idly grouping flowers, and following out her sorrowful thoughts. It was the Dixons. Instead of keeping their holiday by lying in bed, they and their children had roused themselves, and had come by the omnibus to the nearest point. For an instant the meeting was an awkward one, on account of the feud between Margaret Hall and Mrs Dixon, but there was no long resisting of kindly mother Nature's soothings, at that holiday time, and in that lovely tranquil spot; or if they could have been unheeded, the sight of Franky would have awed every angry feeling into rest, so changed was he since the Dixons had last seen him; and since he had been the Puck or Robin Goodfellow of the neighbourhood, whose marbles were always rolling under other people's feet, and whose top−strings were always hanging in nooses to catch the unwary. Yes, he, the feeble, mild, almost girlish−looking lad, had once been a merry, happy rogue, and as such often cuffed by Mrs Dixon, the very Mrs Dixon who now stood gazing with the tears in her eyes. Could she, in sight of him, the changed, the fading, keep up a quarrel with his mother?—

'How long hast thou been here?' asked Dixon.

'Welly on for all day,' answered Libbie.

'Hast never been to see the deer, or the king and queen oaks? Lord, how stupid.'

His wife pinched his arm, to remind him of Franky's helpless condition, which of course tethered the otherwise willing feet. But Dixon had a remedy. He called Bob, and one or two others, and each taking a corner of the strong plaid shawl, they slung Franky as in a hammock, and thus carried him merrily along, down the wood paths, over the smooth, grassy turf, while the glimmering shine and shadow fell on his upturned face. The women walked behind, talking, loitering along, always in sight of the hammock; now picking up some green treasure from the ground, now catching at the low hanging branches of the horse– chestnut. The soul grew much on this day, and in these woods, and all unconsciously, as souls do grow. They followed Franky's hammock–bearers up a grassy knoll, on the top of which stood a group of pine trees, whose stems looked like dark red gold in the sunbeams. They had taken Franky there to show him Manchester, far away in the blue plain, against which the woodland foreground cut with a soft clear line. Far, far away in the distance on that flat plain, you might see the motionless cloud of smoke hanging over a great town, and that was Manchester,—ugly, smoky Manchester, dear, busy, earnest, noble–working Manchester; where their children had been born, and where, perhaps, some lay buried; where their homes were, and where God had cast their lives; and told them to work out their destiny.

'Hurrah! for oud smoke–jack!' cried Bob, putting Franky softly down on the grass, before he whirled his hat round, preparatory to a shout. 'Hurrah! hurrah!' from all the men. 'There's the rim of my hat lying like a quoit yonder,' observed Bob quietly, as he replaced his brimless hat on his head with the gravity of a judge.

'Here's the Sunday–school children a–coming to sit on this shady side, and have their buns and milk. Hark! they're singing the infant–school grace.'

They sat close at hand, so that Franky could hear the words they sang, in rings of children, making, in their gay summer prints, newly donned for that week, garlands of little faces, all happy and bright upon that green hillside. One little 'Dot' of a girl came shyly behind Franky, whom she had long been watching, and threw her half–bun at his side, and then ran away and bid herself, in very shame at the boldness of her own sweet impulse. She kept peeping from her screen at Franky all the time; and—he meanwhile was almost too much pleased and happy to cat; the world was so beautiful, and men, women, and children all so tender, and kind; so softened, in fact, by the beauty of this earth, so unconsciously touched by the spirit of love, which was the Creator of this lovely earth. But the day drew to an end; the heat declined; the birds once more began their warblings; the fresh scents again hung about plant, and tree, and grass, betokening the fragrant presence of the reviving dew and—the boat time was near. As they trod the meadow–path once more, they were joined by many a party they had encountered during the day, all abounding in happiness, all full of the day's adventures, Long–cherished quarrels had been forgotten, new friendships formed. Fresh tastes and higher delights had been imparted that day. We have all of us our look, now and then, called up by some noble or loving thought (our highest on earth), which will be our likeness in heaven. I can catch the, glance on many a face, the glancing light of the cloud of glory from heaven, 'which is our home.' That look was present on many a hard–worked, wrinkled countenance, as they turned backwards to catch a longing, lingering look at Dunham woods, fast deepening into blackness of night, but whose memory was to haunt, in greenness and freshness, many a loom, and workshop, and factory, with images of peace and beauty.

That night, as Libbie lay awake, revolving the incidents of the day, she caught Franky's voice through the open windows. Instead of the frequent moan of pain, he was trying to recall the burden of one of the children's hymns,—

Here we suffer grief and pain, Here we meet to part again; In Heaven we part no more. Oh! that will be joyful,

She recalled his question, the whispered question, to her, in the happiest part of the day. He asked Libbie, 'Is Dunham like heaven? the people here are as kind as angels, and I don't want heaven to be more beautiful than this place. If you and mother would but die with me, I should like to die, and live always there!' She had checked him, for she feared he was impious; but now the young child's craving for some definite idea of the land to which his inner wisdom told him he was hastening, had nothing in it wrong, or even sorrowful, for —

In Heaven we par t no more.

ERA III. MICHAELMAS

The church clocks had struck three; the crowds of gentlemen returning to business, after their early dinners, had disappeared within offices and warehouses; the streets were clear and quiet, and ladies were venturing to sally forth for their afternoon shoppings and their afternoon calls.

Slowly, slowly, along the streets, elbowed by life at every turn, a little funeral wound its quiet way. Four men bore along a child's coffin; two women with bowed heads followed meekly.

I need not tell you whose coffin it was, or who were those two mourners. All was now over with little Frank Hall: his romps, his games, his sickening, his suffering, his death. All was now over, but the Resurrection and the Life.

His mother walked as in a stupor. Could it be that he was dead! If he had been less of an object of her thoughts, less of a motive for her labours, she could sooner have realized it. As it was, she followed his poor, cast-off, worn-out body as if she were borne along by some oppressive dream. If he were really dead, how could she be still alive?

Libbie's mind was far less stunned, and consequently far more active, than Margaret Hall's. Visions, as in a phantasmagoria, came rapidly passing before her—recollections of the time (which seemed now so long ago) when the shadow of the feebly- waving arm first caught her attention; of the bright, strangely isolated day at Dunham Park, where the world had seemed so full of enjoyment, and beauty, and life; of the long-continued heat, through which poor Franky had panted away his strength in the little close room, where there was no escaping the hot rays of the afternoon sun; of the long nights when his mother and she had watched by his side, as he moaned continually, whether awake or asleep; of the fevered moaning slumber of exhaustion; of the pitiful, little self-upbraidings for his own impatience of suffering, only impatient in his own eyes—most true and holy patience in the sight of others; and then the fading away of life, the loss of power, the increased unconsciousness, the lovely look of angelic peace, which followed the dark shadow on the countenance, where was he—what was he now?

And so they laid him in his grave, and beard the solemn funeral words; but far off in the distance, as if not addressed to them.

Margaret Hall bent over the grave to catch one last glance—she had not spoken, nor sobbed, nor done aught but shiver now and then, since the morning; but now her weight bore more heavily on Libbie's arm, and without sigh or sound she fell an unconscious heap on the piled−up gravel. They helped Libbie to bring her round; but long after her half−opened eyes and altered breathings showed that her senses were restored, she lay, speechless and motionless, without attempting to rise from her strange bed, as if the earth contained nothing worth even that trifling exertion.

At last Libbie and she left that holy, consecrated spot, and bent their steps back to the only place more consecrated still; where he had rendered up his spirit; and where memories of him haunted each common, rude piece of furniture that their eyes fell upon. As the woman of the house opened the door, she pulled Libbie on one side, and said—

'Anne Dixon has been across to see you; she wants to have a word with you.'

'I cannot go now,' replied Libbie, as she pushed hastily along, in order to enter the room (his room), at the same time with the childless mother: for, as she had anticipated, the sight of that empty spot, the glance at the uncurtained open window, letting in the fresh air, and the broad, rejoicing light of day, where all had so long been darkened and subdued, unlocked the waters of the fountain, and long and shrill were the cries for her boy that the poor woman uttered.

'Oh! dear Mrs Hall,' said Libbie, herself drenched in tears, 'do not take on so badly; I'm sure it would grieve him sore if he were alive, and you know he is—Bible tells us so; and maybe he's here watching how we go on without him, and hoping we don't fret over−much.'

Mrs Hall's sobs grew worse and more hysterical.

'Oh! listen,' said Libbie, once more struggling against her own increasing agitation. 'Listen! there's Peter chirping as he always does when he's put about, frightened like; and you know he that's gone could never abide to hear the canary chirp in that shrill way.'

Libbie Marsh's Three Eras

Margaret Hall did check herself, and curb her expressions of agony, in order not to frighten the little creature he had loved; and as her outward grief subsided, Libbie took up the large old Bible, which fell open at the never–failing comfort of the fourteenth chapter of St John's Gospel.

How often these large family Bibles do open at that chapter! as if, unused in more joyous and prosperous times, the soul went home to its words of loving sympathy when weary and sorrowful, just as the little child seeks the tender comfort of its mother in all its griefs and cares.

And Margaret put back her wet, ruffled, grey hair from her heated, tear–stained, woeful face, and listened with such earnest eyes, trying to form some idea of the 'Father's house,' where her boy had gone to dwell.

They were interrupted by a low tap at the door. Libbie went. 'Anne Dixon has watched you home, and wants to have a word with you,' said the woman of the house, in a whisper. Libbie went back and closed the book, with a word of explanation to Margaret Hall, and then ran downstairs, to learn the reason of Anne's anxiety to see her.

'Oh, Libbie!' she burst out with, and then, checking herself with the remembrance of Libbie's last solemn duty, 'how's Margaret Hall? But, of course, poor thing, she'll fret a bit at first; she'll be some time coming round, mother says, seeing it's as well that poor lad is taken, for he'd always ha' been a cripple, and a trouble to her—he was a fine lad once, too.'

She had come full of another and a different subject; but the sight of Libbie's sad, weeping face, and the quiet, subdued tone of her manner, made her feel it awkward to begin on any other theme than the one which filled up her companion's mind. To her last speech Libbie answered sorrowfully—

'No doubt, Anne, it's ordered for the best; but oh! don't call him, don't think he could ever ha', been, a trouble to his mother, though he were a cripple. She loved him all the more for each thing she had to do for him—I am sure I did.' Libbie cried a little behind her apron. Anne Dixon felt still more awkward in introducing the discordant subject.

'Well! "flesh is grass," Bible says,' and having fulfilled the etiquette of quoting a text if possible, if not of making a moral observation on the fleeting nature of earthly things, she thought she was at liberty to pass on to her real errand.

'You must not go on moping yourself, Libbie Marsh. What I wanted special for to see you this afternoon, was to tell you, you must come to my wedding tomorrow. Nanny Dawson has fallen sick, and there's none as I should like to have bridesmaid in her place as well as you.'

'Tomorrow! Oh, I cannot!—indeed I cannot!'

'Why not?'

Libbie did not answer, and Anne Dixon grew impatient.

'Surely, in the name o' goodness, you're never going to baulk yourself of a day's pleasure for the sake of yon little cripple that's dead and gone!'

'No,—it's not baulking myself of—don't be angry, Anne Dixon, with him, please; but I don't think it would be a pleasure to me,—I don't feel as if I could enjoy it; thank you all the same. But I did love that little lad very dearly—I did,' sobbing a little, 'and I can't forget him and make merry so soon.'

'Well—I never!' exclaimed Anne, almost angrily.

'Indeed, Anne, I feel your kindness, and you and Bob have my best wishes,—that's what you have; but even if I went, I should be thinking all day of him, and of his poor, poor mother, and they say it's bad to think very much on them that's dead, at a wedding.'

'Nonsense,' said Anne, 'I'll take the risk of the ill−luck. After all, what is marrying? Just a spree, Bob says. He often says he does not think I shall make him a good wife, for I know nought about house matters, wi' working in a factory; but he says he'd rather be uneasy wi' me than easy wi' anybody else. There's love for you! And I tell him I'd rather have him tipsy than anyone else sober.'

Libbie Marsh's Three Eras

'Oh! Anne Dixon, hush! you don't know yet what it is to have a drunken husband. I have seen something of it: father used to get fuddled, and, in the long run, it killed mother, let alone—oh! Anne, God above only knows what the wife of a drunken man has to bear. Don't tell,' said she, lowering her voice, 'but father killed our little baby in one of his bouts; mother never looked up again, nor father either, for that matter, only his was in a different way. Mother will have gotten to little Jemmie now, and they'll be so happy together,—and perhaps Franky too. Oh!' said she, recovering herself from her train of thought, .never say aught lightly of the wife's lot whose husband is given to drink!'

'Dear, what a preachment. I tell you what, Libbie, you're as born an old maid as ever I saw. You'll never be married to either drunken or sober.'

Libbie's face went rather red, but without losing its meek expression.

'I know that as well as you can tell me; and more reason, therefore, as God has seen fit to keep me out of woman's natural work, I should try and find work for myself. I mean,' seeing Anne Dixon's puzzled look, 'that as I know I'm never likely to have a home of my own, or a husband that would look to me to make all straight, or children to watch over or care for, all which I take to be woman's natural work, I must not lose time in fretting and fidgetting after marriage, but just look about me for somewhat else to do. I can see many a one misses it in this. They will banker after what is ne'er likely to be theirs, instead of facing it out, and settling down to be old maids; and, as old maids, just looking round for the odd jobs God leaves in the world for such as old maids to do. There's plenty of such work, and there's the blessing of God on them as does it.' Libbie was almost out of breath at this outpouring of what had long been her inner thoughts.

'That's all very true, I make no doubt, for them as is to be old maids; but as I'm not, please God tomorrow comes, you might have spared your breath to cool your porridge. What I want to know is, whether you'll be bridesmaid tomorrow or not. Come, now do; it will do you good, after all your working, and watching, and slaying yourself for that poor Franky Hall.'

'It was one of my odd jobs,' said Libbie, smiling, though her eyes were brimming over with tears; 'but, dear Anne,' said she, recovering herself, 'I could not do it tomorrow, indeed I could not.'

Libbie Marsh's Three Eras

'And I can't wait,' said Anne Dixon, almost sulkily, 'Bob and I put it off from today, because of the funeral, and Bob had set his heart on its being on Michaelmas Day; and mother says the goose won't keep beyond tomorrow. Do come: father finds eatables, and Bob finds drink, and we shall be so jolly! and after we've been to church, we're to walk round the town in pairs, white satin ribbon in our bonnets, and refreshments at any public−house we like, Bob says. And after dinner there's to be a dance. Don't be a fool; you can do no good by staying. Margaret Hall will have to go out washing, I'll be bound.'

'Yes, she must go to Mrs Wilkinson's, and, for that matter, I must go working too. Mrs Williams has been after me to make her girl's winter things ready; only I could not leave Franky, he clung so to me.'

'Then you won't be bridesmaid! is that your last word?'

'It is; you must not be angry with me, Anne Dixon,' said Libbie, deprecatingly.

But Anne was gone without a reply.

With a heavy heart Libbie mounted the little staircase, for she felt how ungracious her refusal of Anne's kindness must appear, to one who understood so little the feelings which rendered her acceptance of it a moral impossibility.

On opening the door she saw Margaret Hall, with the Bible open on the table before her. For she had puzzled out the place where Libbie was reading, and, with her finger under the line, was spelling out the words of consolation, piecing the syllables together aloud, with the earnest anxiety of comprehension with which a child first learns to read. So Libbie took the stool by her side, before she was aware that anyone had entered the room.

'What did she want you for?' asked Margaret. 'But I can guess; she wanted you to be at th' wedding that is to come off this week, they say. Ay, they'll marry, and laugh, and dance, all as one as if my boy was alive,' said she, bitterly. 'Well, he was neither kith nor kin of yours, so I maun try and be thankful for what you've done for him, and not wonder at your forgetting him afore he's well settled in his grave.'

'I never can forget him, and I'm not going to the wedding,' said Libbie, quietly, for she understood the mother's jealousy of her dead child's claims.

Libbie Marsh's Three Eras

'I must go work at Mrs Williams' tomorrow,' she said, in explanation, for she was unwilling to boast of her tender, fond regret, which had been her principal motive for declining Anne's invitation.

'And I mun go washing, just as if nothing had happened,' sighed forth Mrs Hall, 'and I mun come home at night, and find his place empty, and all still where I used to be sure of hearing his voice ere ever I got up the stair: no one will ever call me mother again.' She fell crying pitifully, and Libbie could not speak for her own emotion for some time. But during this silence she put the keystone in the arch of thoughts she had been building up for many days; and when Margaret was again calm in her sorrow, Libbie said. 'Mrs Hall, I should like— would you like me to come for to live here altogether?'

Margaret Hall looked up with a sudden light in her countenance, which encouraged Libbie to go on.

'I could sleep with you, and pay half, you know; and we should be together in the evenings; and her as was home first would watch for the other, and' (dropping her voice) 'we could talk of him at nights, you know.'

She was going on, but Mrs Hall interrupted her.

'Oh, Libbie Marsh! and can you really think of coming to live wi' me. I should like it above—but no! it must not be; you've no notion on what a creature I am, at times; more like a mad one when I'm in a rage, and I cannot keep it down. I seem to get out of bed wrong side in the morning, and I must have my passion out with the first person I meet. Why, Libbie,' said she, with a doleful look of agony on her face, 'I even used to fly out on him, poor sick lad as he was, and you may judge how little you can keep it down frae that. No, you must not come. I must live alone now,' sinking her voice into the low tones of despair.

But Libbie's resolution was brave and strong. 'I'm not afraid,' said she smiling. 'I know you better than you know yourself, Mrs Hail. I've seen you try of late to keep it down, when you've been boiling over, and I think you'll go on a–doing so. And at any rate, when you've had your fit out, you're very kind, and I can forget if you've been a bit put out. But I'll try not to put you out. Do let me come: I think he would like us to keep together. I'll do my very best to make you comfortable.'

25

Libbie Marsh's Three Eras

'It's me! it's me as will be making your life miserable with my temper; or else, God knows, how my heart clings to you. You and me is folk alone in the world, for we both loved one who is dead, and who had none else to love him. If you will live with me, Libbie, I'll try as I never did afore to be gentle and quiet–tempered, Oh! will you try me, Libbie Marsh?' So out of the little grave there sprang a hope and a resolution, which made life an object to each of the two.

When Elizabeth Marsh returned home the next evening from her day's labours, Anne (Dixon no longer) crossed over, all in her bridal finery, to endeavour to induce her to join the dance going on in her, father's house.

'Dear Anne, this is good of you, a–thinking of me tonight,' said Libbie, kissing her, 'and though I cannot come,—I've promised Mrs Hall to be with her,—I shall think on you, and I trust you'll be happy. I have got a little needle–case I have looked out for you; stay, here it is,—I wish it were more—only — '

'Only, I know what. You've been a–spending all your money in nice things for poor Franky. Thou'rt a real good un, Libbie, and I'll keep your needle–book to my dying day, that I will.' Seeing Anne in such a friendly mood, emboldened Libbie to tell her of her change of place; of her intention of lodging henceforward with Margaret Hall.

'Thou never will! Why father and mother are as fond of thee as can be; they'll lower thy rent if that's what it is—and thou knowst they never grudge thee bit or drop. And Margaret Hall, of all folk, to lodge. wi'! She's such a Tartar! Sooner than not have a quarrel, she'd fight right hand against left. Thou'lt have no peace of thy life. What on earth can make you think of such a thing, Libbie Marsh?'

'She'll be so lonely without me,' pleaded Libbie. 'I'm sure I could make her happier, even if she did scold me a bit now and then, than she'd be a living alone, and I'm not afraid of her; and I mean to do my best not to vex her: and it will case her heart, maybe, to talk to me at times about Franky. I shall often see your father and mother, and I shall always thank them for their kindness to me. But they have you and little Mary, and poor Mrs Hall has no one.'

Anne could only repeat, 'Well, I never!' and hurry off to tell the news at home.

Libbie Marsh's Three Eras

But Libbie was right. Margaret Hall is a different woman to the scold of the neighbourhood she once was; touched and softened by the two purifying angels, Sorrow and Love. And it is beautiful to see her affection, her reverence, for Libbie Marsh. Her dead mother could hardly have cared for her more tenderly than does the hardhearted washerwoman, not long ago so fierce and unwomanly. Libbie, herself, has such peace shining on her countenance, as almost makes it beautiful, as she tenders the services of a daughter to Franky's mother, no longer the desolate lonely orphan, a stranger on the earth.

Do you ever read the moral, concluding sentence of a story? I never do, but I once (in the year 1811, I think) heard of a deaf old lady, living by herself, who did; and as she may have left some descendants with the same amiable peculiarity, I will put in, for their benefit, what I believe to be the secret of Libbie's peace of mind, the real reason why she no longer feels oppressed at her own loneliness in the world,—

She has a purpose in life; and that purpose is a holy one.

CPSIA information can be obtained at www.ICGtesting.com
Printed in the USA
BVOW061021220113

311274BV00012B/278/P